Read for a Better World™

THE FIRST DAY OF SCHOOL

MARGO GATES

GRL Consultants,
Diane Craig and Monica Marx,
Certified Literacy Specialists

Lerner Publications ◆ Minneapolis

TABLE OF CONTENTS

The First Day of School

We pack our backpacks and put on our shoes. We are ready for the first day of school!

Some of us ride
the bus to school.
Some of us bike
or walk.

How do you get
to school?

Our teacher meets
us at the door.
She tells us where
to go.

This is our classroom.
We meet our new
classmates.

Our teacher shows us around the school. Here is the gym.

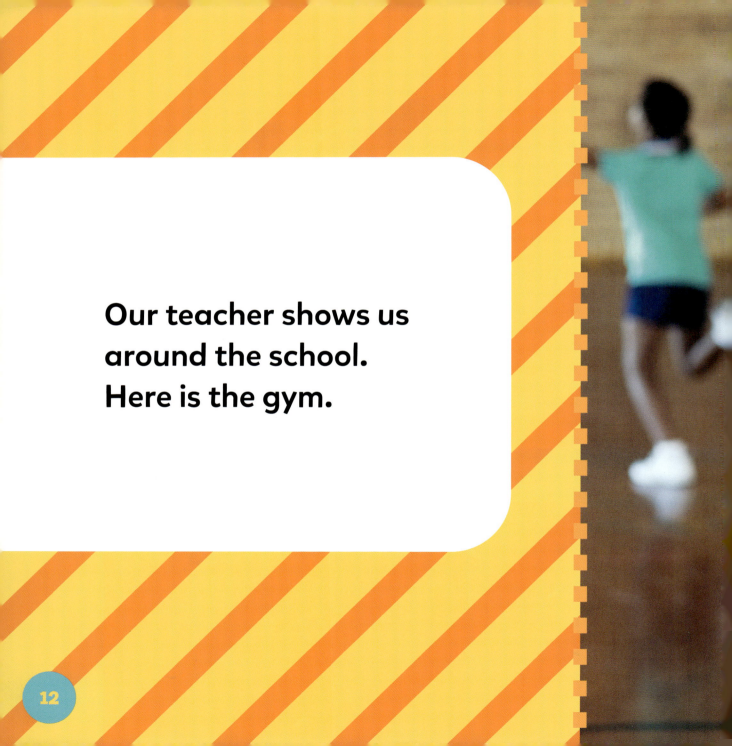

It is time for lunch!
We eat in the
lunchroom.

After lunch is recess.
We run and play.

What do you like to do at recess?

We go back to
the classroom.
We learn to read
and write.

It is time to go home.
We can't wait to come back tomorrow!

You Connect!

What is something you did on your first day of school?

Who is someone you met on your first day of school?

How did you feel on the first day of school?

Social and Emotional Snapshot

Student voice is crucial to building reader confidence. Ask the reader:

> What is your favorite part of this book?

> What is something you learned from this book?

> Did this book remind you of your own first day of school?

Opportunities for social and emotional learning are everywhere. How can you connect the topic of this book to the SEL competencies below?

Self-Awareness
Relationship Skills
Social Awareness

Photo Glossary

backpack

bus

gym

teacher

Learn More

Bullard, Lisa. *Sofia's First Day of School*. Minneapolis: Millbrook Press, 2018.

Gates, Margo. *The 100th Day of School*. Minneapolis: Lerner Publications, 2023.

Rabe, Tish. *On the First Day of First Grade*. New York: Harper, 2018.

Index

Photo Acknowledgments

The images in this book are used with the permission of: © FatCamera/iStockphoto, p. 17; © kali9/iStockphoto, pp. 6, 23 (bus); © Monkey Business Images/Shutterstock Images, pp. 4–5, 10–11, 16, 23 (backpack); © monkeybusinessimages/iStockphoto, p. 20; © romrodinka/iStockphoto, pp. 6–7; © skynesher/iStockphoto, pp. 8–9; © SolStock/iStockphoto, pp. 14–15, 18–19, 23 (teacher); © Wavebreakmedia/iStockphoto, pp. 12–13, 23 (gym).

Cover Photo: wavebreakmedia/Shutterstock Images.

Design Elements: © Mighty Media, Inc.

Lerner Publications Company
An imprint of Lerner Publishing Group, Inc.
241 First Avenue North
Minneapolis, MN 55401 USA

For reading levels and more information, look up this title at www.lernerbooks.com.

Main body text set in Mikado a Medium.
Typeface provided by Hannes von Doehren.

Library of Congress Cataloging-in-Publication Data

Names: Gates, Margo, author.
Title: The first day of school / Margo Gates.
Description: Minneapolis : Lerner Publications, 2023. | Series: Read about school (Read for a better world) | Audience: Ages 5–8 | Audience: Grades K–1 | Summary: "The first day of school is all about meeting new people and learning new routines. Readers preparing to start a new school year will enjoy this look at what to expect on Day One"– Provided by publisher.
Identifiers: LCCN 2021043330 (print) | LCCN 2021043331 (ebook) | ISBN 9781728459271 (library binding) | ISBN 9781728461830 (ebook)
Subjects: LCSH: First day of school—Juvenile literature.
Classification: LCC LB1556 .G37 2023 (print) | LCC LB1556 (ebook) | DDC 37.1—dc23

LC record available at https://lccn.loc.gov/2021043330
LC ebook record available at https://lccn.loc.gov/2021043331

Manufactured in the United States of America
1 – CG – 7/15/22